男人与女人

Men & Women

李溪 编译

外文出版社

图书在版编目（CIP）数据

男人与女人/李湲编译. —北京：外文出版社，2005（笑话集锦）
ISBN 7-119-04247-5

Ⅰ. 男... Ⅱ. 李... Ⅲ. 英语-对照读物，笑话-英、汉
Ⅳ. H319.4：Ⅰ

中国版本图书馆 CIP 数据核字（2005）第 111269 号

外文出版社网址：
  http://www.flp.com.cn
外文出版社电子信箱：
  info@flp.com.cn
  sales@flp.com.cn

笑话集锦
男人与女人

编　译　李　湲

责任编辑　李春英
封面设计　李迎迎
印刷监制　冯　浩
出版发行　外文出版社
社　　址　北京市百万庄大街 24 号　　邮政编码　100037
电　　话　（010）68995883（编辑部）
　　　　　（010）68329514/68327211（推广发行部）
印　　刷　三河汇鑫印务有限公司
经　　销　新华书店/外文书店
开　　本　32 开　　　　　　　字　　数　30 千字
印　　数　5001—10000 册　　　印　　张　6.25
版　　次　2006 年第 1 版第 2 次印刷
装　　别　平
书　　号　ISBN 7-119-04247-5
定　　价　9.80 元

目 录
Contents

There are 2 times when a man doesn't understand a woman: before marriage & after.

男人有两个时期不了解女人，结婚前和结婚后。

Love Letter

Dear Thomas:

I want a man who knows what love is all about. You are generous, kind, thoughtful. People who are not like you admit to being useless and inferior.

You have ruined me for other men. I yearn for you. I have no feelings whatsoever when we're apart. I can be forever happy — will you let me be yours?

Maria

情　书

亲爱的托马斯：

　　我想要的是一个真正懂得爱的人。你宽宏、善良、体贴。只有你这样的人才是有用的人和高贵的人。

　　你使我无法接受其他的人。我无时无刻不思慕着你。我们不在一起时，我根本就毫无感情。我会永远幸福——让我和你在一起吧，好吗？

　　　　　　　　　　　　　　　　　　玛利亚

Dear Thomas:

I want a man who knows what love is. All about you are generous, kind, thoughtful people, who are not like you. Admit to being useless and inferior.

You have ruined me. For other men, I yearn. For you, I have no feelings whatsoever. When we're apart, I can be forever happy. Will you let me be?

Yours, Maria

男人与女人

亲爱的托马斯：

我想要的是一个真正懂得爱的人。他要宽宏、善良、体贴，而你不是这样的。你低能而窝囊。

你毁了我。我思慕着别的人。我对你没有任何的感觉。不和你在一起时，我会很快乐。请你放了我吧，好吗？

玛利亚

☆ **generous** /ˈdʒenərəs/ *a.* 慷慨的；宽厚的

☆ **thoughtful** /ˈθɔːtful/ *a.* 体贴的；考虑周到的

☆ **yearn** /jɜːn/ *v.* 渴望；怀念；思慕；向往

☆ **whatsoever** /ˌhwɒtsəʊˈevə(r)/ *a.* (= at all) 丝毫的，任何的

Frog Prince

Once upon a time, a beautiful, independent, self-assured princess happened upon a frog in a pond.

The frog said to the princess, "I was once a handsome prince until an evil witch put a spell on me. One kiss from you and I will turn back into a prince and then we can marry, move into the castle with my mom and you can prepare my meals, clean my clothes, bear my children and forever feel happy doing so."

That night, while the princess dined on frog legs, she kept laughing and saying, "I don't think so."

青蛙王子

从前，一位漂亮、独立、自信的公主遇到了池塘里的一只青蛙。

青蛙对公主说："我曾经是位英俊的王子，一个邪恶的女巫用咒语把我变成了这个样子。你的一个吻就能让我变回王子，然后你就嫁给我，搬到城堡里和我妈妈一起住。你可以为我准备饭菜，帮我洗衣服，给我生孩子，这样永远幸福地生活在一起。"

那天晚上，公主吃着青蛙腿时，还止不住地笑着说："我可不这么想。"

☆ **independent** /ˌɪndɪ'pendənt/ *a.* 独立的；有主见的

☆ **self-assured** /ˌselfə'ʃuəd/ *a.* 自信的，自持的

☆ **happen upon** 偶然遇到；偶然发现

Tiny Men and Tiny Women

What is a CAT?

1. Cats do what they want.

2. They rarely listen to you.

3. They're totally unpredictable.

4. When you want to play, they want to be alone.

5. When you want to be alone, they want to play.

6. They expect you to cater to their every whim.

7. They're moody.

8. They leave hair everywhere.

CONCLUSION: They're tiny women in little fur coats.

男
人
与
女
人

小男人和小女人

猫是什么?

1. 猫们随心所欲。

2. 猫们极少听你的话。

3. 它们完全不可捉摸。

4. 你想玩耍的时候,它们想独个待着。

5. 你想一个人待着时,它们想要玩耍。

6. 它们希望你能迎合它们心血来潮的念头。

7. 它们喜怒无常。

8. 它们到处掉毛。

结论: 它们是披着小号毛皮外套的小号的女人。

What is a DOG?

1. Dogs spend all day sprawled on the most comfortable piece of furniture in the house.

2. They can hear a package of food opening half a block away, but don't hear you when you're in the same room.

3. They can look dumb and lovable all at the same time.

4. They growl when they are not happy.

5. When you want to play, they want to play.

6. When you want to be alone, they want to play.

7. They leave their toys everywhere.

CONCLUSION: They're tiny men in little fur coats.

狗是什么？

1. 狗们整天整天地赖在家里最舒服的家具上。

2. 它们能听到半个街区外开食品袋的声音，可是你和它在同一间屋里它倒听不见。

3. 同一时间，它们能显得又笨又可爱。

4. 它们不高兴时就会乱吼。

5. 你想玩耍时，它们也想玩耍。

6. 你想一个人待着时，它们想要玩耍。

7. 它们把玩具到处乱扔。

结论：他们是披着小号毛皮外套的小号的男人。

☆ **unpredictable** /ˌʌnprɪˈdɪktəbl/ *a.* 不定的，易变的

☆ **cater to** 满足需要（或欲望）；投合，迎合

☆ **sprawl** /sprɔːl/ *v.* （懒散地）伸开四肢躺（或坐）

☆ **growl** /ɡraʊl/ *v.* 狂吠；发低沉的怒声；咆哮

Woman Dentist

"I would like to see a woman dentist," said a man.

"Why?" asked his friend.

"Because it would be a pleasure to have a woman say, 'open your mouth' instead of 'shut up!'"

男人与女人

女 牙 医

"我想找一个女牙医。"一个男人说。

"为什么呢?"他的朋友问道。

"因为听一个女人说'张开你的嘴'总比听她说'闭嘴!'要令人愉快得多。"

A Sudden Change of Mind

My Dearest Susan,

Sweetie of my heart. I've been so desolate ever since I broke off our engagement. Simply devastated. Won't you please consider coming back to me? You hold a place in my heart no other woman can fill. I can never marry another woman quite like you. I need you so much. Won't you forgive me and let us make a new beginning? I love you so.

Yours always and truly,

John

P. S. Congratulations on you winning the state lottery.

突然改变主意

最亲爱的苏珊：

　　我的宝贝。我推掉我们的婚约后孑然一身，完全的身心交瘁。你能否考虑回到我的身边？你在我心中的地位没有其他女人可以替代。我再也不会找到一个像你这样的女人了。我太需要你了。你能不能原谅我，让我们重新开始？我爱你。

你永远真挚的
约翰

又及：祝贺你在全国彩票中中大奖。

☆ **desolate** /ˈdesələt/ *a.* 被遗弃的；孤独凄凉的

☆ **break off** 绝交，断绝友好关系

☆ **engagement** /ɪnˈɡeɪdʒmənt/ *v.* 订婚，婚约

☆ **devastate** /ˈdevəsteɪt/ *v.* 压倒，使垮掉

☆ **P. S.** （postscript）（信末签名后的）附笔，又及

☆ **lottery** /ˈlɒtərɪ/ *n.* 抽彩给奖法

Men's Rules

If Men Were to Rewrite "The Rules"

Rule 1 Anything we said several months ago is inadmissible in an argument. All comments become null and void after seven days.

Rule 2 If we say something that can be interpreted in two ways, and one of the ways makes you sad or angry, we meant the other way.

Rule 3 It is in neither your best interest nor ours to make us take those stupid Cosmo quizzes together.

Rule 4 You can either ask us to do something OR tell us how you want it done — not both.

Rule 5 Whenever possible, please say whatever you have to say during commercials or time-outs.

男人与女人

男人制定的规则

如果男人们能够重写"规则"

规则一 吵架中，我们几个月以前说过的话是不能作为证据的。我们说过的所有的话在七天后就无效。

规则二 如果我们说的话有两种理解方式，而且其中的一种会让你们难过或生气，我们的话想表达的意思就是另外那种。

规则三 一起做《时尚》杂志上那些愚蠢的字谜游戏，既不是你们最大的乐趣也不是我们的。

规则四 你们可以或者让我们做什么事或者告诉我们你们想要这件事怎样做——不要两样都说。

规则五 只要有可能，请在播放广告期间或中场休息时说你们一定要说的话。

Rule 6　Christopher Columbus didn't need directions and neither do we.

Rule 7　When we're turning the wheel and the car is nosing onto the ramp, you saying "This is our exit" is not necessary.

规则六 克里斯托弗·哥伦布不需要人指路，我们也一样。

规则七 当我们已经转方向盘，把车开上坡道时，你就没必要说"这是出口"了。

☆ **inadmissible** /ˌɪnəd'mɪsəbl/ *a*. 不许可的；（证据等）不可接受的；不能承认的

☆ **argument** /'ɑːgjʊmənt/ *n*. 争论，争吵；辩论

☆ **comment** /'kɒment/ *n*. 批评，意见；评论；闲话

☆ **null and void** （法律上）无效的，无束缚力的

☆ **interpret** /ɪn'tɜːprɪt/ *v*. 解释，说明；理解

☆ **ramp** /ræmp/ *n*. （机动车、轮椅等使用的）坡道

19

Some Truth

A man will pay $2 for a $1 item he wants.

A woman will pay $1 for a $2 item that she doesn't want.

A man never worries about the future until he gets a wife.

A woman worries about the future until she gets a husband.

A successful man is one who makes more money than his wife can spend.

A successful woman is one who can find such a man.

To be happy with a man you must understand him a lot & love him a little.

一些事实

男人会花两块钱买一件价值一块钱的东西，因为这是他想要的东西。

女人会花一块钱买到一件价值两块钱的东西，但这并不是她想要的。

男人在没有结婚前不会为将来操心。

女人在结婚后就不再为将来操心。

一个成功的男人赚的钱要比他老婆能花掉的多。

一个成功的女人要能找到这样的男人。

和男人幸福相处的秘诀是更多地了解他，但要少爱他一些。

To be happy with a woman you must love her a lot & not try to understand her at all.

Men wake up as good-looking as they went to bed.

Women somehow deteriorate during the night.

A man marries a woman expecting that she won't change and she does.

A woman marries a man expecting he will change, but he doesn't.

A woman has the last word in any argument.

Anything a man says after that is the beginning of a new argument.

男人与女人

和女人幸福相处的秘诀是更多地爱她，但根本不要试图去了解她。

男人起床时的样子和他上床时的样子一样。

女人睡了一晚之后多多少少变了样子。

男人娶女人时希望她不会改变，可她偏偏就变了。

女人嫁给男人时希望他有所改变，可他偏偏就变不了。

每次吵架总是女人收尾。

男人在那之后说的话会导致新一轮吵架的开始。

☆ **deteriorate** /dɪˈtɪəriəreɪt/ *v.* 恶化；质量（或价值）下降

23

A Woman's Guide to
What a Man Is Really Saying

I'M HUNGRY.

I'm hungry.

I'M SLEEPY.

I'm sleepy.

I'M TIRED.

I'm tired.

WHAT'S WRONG?

I don't see why you're making such a big deal out of this.

WHAT'S WRONG?

男人话语隐含意义指南

我饿了。

我饿了。

我困了。

我困了。

我累了。

我累了。

出什么事了？

我不知道你为什么要这么小题大做。

出什么事了？

25

What meaningless self-inflicted psycho-logical trauma are you going through now?

YES, I LIKE THE WAY YOU CUT YOUR HAIR.

I liked it better before.

YES, I LIKE THE WAY YOU CUT YOUR HAIR.

$50 and it doesn't look that much different!

YES, I LIKE THE WAY YOU CUT YOUR HAIR.

For $50 they should have GIVEN YOU hair!

你又在那儿无病呻吟什么呢?

是的，我喜欢你的新发型。

我还是比较喜欢你原来的发型。

是的，我喜欢你的新发型。

50 块钱！这和以前看起来没多大不同！

是的，我喜欢你的新发型。

50 块钱！他们该为你剪掉的头发付钱才对！

☆ **make a big deal out of**　极端重视；对…大惊小怪

☆ **meaningless** /ˈmiːnɪŋlɪs/ *a.* 无意义的；无目的的

☆ **self-inflicted** /ˌselfɪnˈflɪktɪd/ *a.* 加于自身的

☆ **psychological** /ˌsaɪkəˈlɒdʒɪkəl/ *a.* 精神的

☆ **trauma** /ˈtrɔːmə/ *n.* 伤口；（心理上的）创伤

☆ **go through**　遭受,经历,经受

A Man's Guide to
What a Woman Is Really Saying

I JUST NEED SOME SPACE.

. . . . without you in it.

DO I LOOK FAT IN THIS DRESS?

We haven't had a fight in a while.

NO, PIZZA'S FINE.

. . . . you cheap slob!

I JUST DON'T WANT A BOYFRIEND NOW.

I just don't want you as a boyfriend now.

I DON'T KNOW. WHAT DO YOU WANT TO

DO?

男人与女人

女人话语隐含意义指南

我需要一些空间。
……没有你在里面。

我穿这身衣服是不是显胖？
我们有段时间没吵架了。

不，不，吃比萨饼就很好。
……你这个抠门的家伙！

我现在还不想交男朋友。
我就是不想你做我男朋友。

我不知道。你想做什么？

I can't believe you have nothing planned.

COME HERE.
My puppy does this, too.

I LIKE YOU, BUT....
I don't like you.

YOU NEVER LISTEN.
You never listen.

I'LL BE READY IN A MINUTE.
I'm ready, but I'm going to make you wait because I know you will.

OH, NO, I'LL PAY FOR MYSELF.
I'm just being nice; there's no way I'm going Dutch.

我简直不敢相信你竟然毫无计划。

过来。
我的小狗也是这样的。

我喜欢你，但是……
我不喜欢你。

你从不听我的话。
你从不听我的话。

我马上就好。
我已经准备好了，可我就是想让你等，因为我知道你会等的。

哦，不用了，我自己付。
我只是想表现一下，想跟我 AA 制，没门。

☆ **There is no way....**　　……没有可能。
☆ **go Dutch**　各人付各人的账；
　　平摊费用

He Said — She Said

He said . . . Do you love me just because my father left me a fortune?

She said . . . Not at all honey, I would love you no matter who left you the money.

He said . . . This coffee isn't fit for a pig!

She said . . . No problem, I'll get you some that is.

She said . . . What do you mean by coming home half drunk?

He said . . . It's not my fault . . . I ran out of money.

他说——她说

他说……你爱我只是因为我爸爸留给我一大笔钱吗?

她说……绝对不是的,不管是谁留给你的那些钱,我都爱你。

他说……这咖啡给猪喝都不行!

她说……没问题,我去给你拿一杯可以给猪喝的。

她说……你喝个半醉回来是什么意思?

他说……这不是我的错,我没钱再喝了。

He said ... Why do you women always try to impress us with your looks, not with your brains?

She said ... Because there is a bigger chance that a man is a moron than he is blind.

He said ... What have you been doing with all the grocery money I gave you?

She said ... Turn sideways and look in the mirror.

He said ... Let's go out and have some fun tonight.

She said ... Okay, but if you get home before I do, leave the hallway light on.

男人与女人

他说……为什么你们女人总是用外表而不是思想来吸引我们呢？

她说……因为男人是傻瓜的几率要比是瞎子的几率高得多。

他说……我给你的家用钱都干什么了？

她说……逛街照镜子。

他说……今晚我们出去玩玩。

她说……好吧，如果你先回家，帮我把过道的灯开着。

Brain Transplant

A patient needed a brain transplant and the doctor told the family, "Brains are very expensive, and you will have to pay the costs yourselves."

"Well, how much does a brain cost?" asked the relatives.

"For a male brain, $500,000. For a female brain, $200,000," replied the doctor.

All the male relatives nodded because they thought they understood.

脑 移 植

一个病人需要进行脑移植，医生对他的家属说："脑器官是很贵的，而且是自费的。"

"那么，一个大脑到底要多少钱呢？"病人家属问道。

"男人的大脑 50 万美元，女人的要 20 万，"医生答道。

病人所有的男性亲属都故作理解地点点头。

But the patient's daughter was unsatisfied and asked, "Why the difference in price between male brains and female brains?"

"Standard pricing practice," said the doctor.

"Men's brains cost more, for they are brand-new and women's brains have to be marked down because they've actually been used."

但是病人的女儿并不满意，问道："男人大脑的价格和女人的为什么差这么多？"

"这是标准的价格规范，"医生说。

"男人的大脑贵是因为它们是全新的，而女人的大脑要价低是因为它们确实是使用过的二手货。"

☆ **transplant** /træns'plɑːnt/ *n.* 【医】移植（器官）

☆ **standard** /'stændəd/ *a.* （符合）标准的

☆ **practice** /'præktɪs/ *n.* 惯常做法，惯例

☆ **brand-new** /'brænd'njuː/ *a.* 全新的，崭新的

☆ **mark down**　削减…的价目，标低…价格

How Old Am I?

Some people grow old gracefully, while others fight and scratch the whole way.

男人与女人

Judy, a friend of my, refusing to give in to the looks of growing old, goes out and buys a new line of expensive cosmetics guaranteed to make her look years younger.

After a lengthy sitting before the mirror applying the "miracle" products, she asks her husband, "Darling, honestly, if you didn't know me, what age would you say I am?"

我多大了？

有人优雅地老去，也有人挣扎着不愿面对岁月流逝的现实。

朱迪，我的一个朋友，不愿屈从于自己的容貌变老而跑去买了一整套价格不菲的据说是能使她显得年轻的新款护肤品。

坐在镜子前长时间地涂涂抹抹这种"神奇的"化妆品后，她问丈夫："亲爱的，你跟我说实话，如果你不认识我，你认为我多大了？"

Looking over her carefully, he replied, "Judging from your skin, twenty; your hair, eighteen; and your figure, twenty five."

"Oh, you flatterer!" she gushed. Just as she was about to tell him his reward, he stops her by saying. . . .

"WHOA, hold on there sweety!" he interrupted. "I haven't added them up yet!"

他仔细地看了看她，说："从你的皮肤判断是20岁；从你的头发看是18岁；看身材嘛，25岁。"

"哎呀，你这个马屁精！"她嗲嗲地说。就在她要说出对他的奖赏时，他打断了她……

"啊啊，亲爱的，打住！"他说，"我还没把这些数字加起来呢！"

☆ **gracefully** /ˈɡreɪsfʊlɪ/ *ad.* 优美地，优雅地

☆ **guarantee** /ˌɡærənˈtiː/ *v.* 保证；确保

☆ **lengthy** /ˈleŋθɪ/ *a.* (讲话，文章等) 冗长乏味的

☆ **apply** /əˈplaɪ/ *v.* 涂；敷；把…施用于

☆ **flatterer** /ˈflætərə(r)/ *n.* 阿谀奉承者，拍马屁的人

☆ **gush** /ɡʌʃ/ *v.* 滔滔地说；装腔作势

☆ **interrupt** /ˌɪntəˈrʌpt/ *v.* 中止；打断

How About My Stone?

Sometime after Paul died, his widow, Lily, was finally able to speak about what a thoughtful and wonderful man her late husband had been.

"Paul thought of everything," she told her friends. "Just before he died, Paul handed me three envelopes. 'Lily,' he told me, 'I have put all my last wishes in these three envelopes. After I am dead, please open them and do exactly as I have instructed. Then, I can rest in peace.'"

"What was in the envelopes?" her friends asked.

我的石头怎么样？

在丈夫保罗去世一段时间之后，莉莉终于能对朋友们讲她的老公是个多么善解人意的好男人了。

"保罗想到了每一件事，"她说，"他死前给了我三个信封，对我说'莉莉，我把我最后的三个心愿放在这三个信封里了。我死后，请你打开它们，按照我说的做，我就能在九泉下安息了。'"

"那些信封里有什么？"她的朋友们问。

"The first envelope contained $5,000 with a note, 'Please use this money to buy a nice casket.' So I bought a beautiful mahogany casket with such a comfortable lining that I know Paul is resting very comfortably."

"The second envelope contained $10,000 with a note, 'Please use this for a nice funeral.' I arranged Paul a very dignified funeral and bought all his favorite foods for everyone attending."

"And the third envelope?" asked her friends.

"第一个信封里有 5000 块钱，还有一张纸条写着，'请用这笔钱买一口上好的棺材。'于是我给他买了一副衬有舒适衬里的上好的红木棺材。我知道保罗躺在里面一定很舒服。"

"第二个信封里有一万块钱，还有一张纸条写着，'请用这笔钱帮我办一个体面的葬礼。'于是我为他办了一个庄严肃穆的葬礼，为所有的来宾准备了他最爱吃的食物。"

"第三个信封呢?"她的朋友们问。

男人与女人

"The third envelope contained ＄30,000 with a note, 'Please use this to buy a nice stone.'"

Holding her hand in the air, Lily said, "So, do you like my stone?" showing off her 10 carat diamond ring.

"第三个信封里有三万块钱，还有一张纸条写着，'请用这笔钱买一块上好的石头（墓碑）。'"

　　莉莉把手举了起来，炫耀着手上 10 克拉的钻石戒指，说："我这块石头怎么样？"

☆ **casket** /ˈkɑːskɪt/ *n.* （尤指昂贵而有华丽装饰的）棺材

☆ **mahogany** /məˈhɒgənɪ/ *a.* 红木做的

☆ **stone** /stəʊn/ *n.* 石头；墓碑；宝石，钻石

What I Want in a Man!

Age 22

1. Handsome.

2. Charming.

3. Financially successful.

4. A caring listener.

5. Witty.

6. In good shape.

7. Dresses with style.

8. Appreciates the finer things.

9. Full of thoughtful surprises.

10. An imaginative, romantic lover.

我想要这样的男人！

22 岁时

1. 英俊。

2. 迷人。

3. 富有。

4. 善解人意的倾听者。

5. 风趣。

6. 身体棒。

7. 衣着时尚。

8. 能够欣赏更完美的事物。

9. 常能给我我想要的惊喜。

10. 富有想像力的、浪漫的情人。

Age 32

1. Nice looking — preferably with hair on his head.

2. Opens car doors，holds chairs.

3. Has enough money for a nice dinner at a restaurant.

4. Listens more then he talks.

5. Laughs at my jokes at appropriate times.

6. Can carry all the groceries with ease.

7. Owns at least one tie.

8. Appreciates a good home cooked meal.

9. Remembers anniversaries.

10. Likes to be romantic at least once a week.

32 岁时

1. 相貌好，最好不是秃头。

2. 为我开车门、拉椅子。

3. 有足够的钱请我去餐馆吃一顿不错的晚餐。

4. 他听我说多过我听他说。

5. 我讲笑话时能适时地用笑回应。

6. 轻松地拿所有的购物袋。

7. 至少有一条领带。

8. 爱吃一道家常饭菜。

9. 记得所有的纪念日。

10. 一星期至少浪漫一次。

Age 42

1. Not too ugly. Bald head OK.

2. Doesn't drive off until I'm in the car.

3. Works steady — splurges on dinner at McDonald's on occasion.

4. Nods head at appropriate times when I'm talking.

5. Usually remembers the punch line of jokes.

6. Is in good enough shape to rearrange the furniture.

7. Usually wears shirt that covers stomach.

8. Knows not to buy champagne with screw top lids.

9. Remembers to put the toilet seat down.

10. Shaves on most weekends.

42 岁时

1. 不要太难看，秃头也将就了。

2. 不会在我还没上车时，就把车开走了。

3. 工作稳定，偶尔挥霍一下带我去吃麦当劳。

4. 我说话时能适时地点头呼应。

5. 总是能记得笑话的关键句。

6. 身体健康，能搬得动家具。

7. 通常穿能够遮住肚皮的衬衫。

8. 知道不买螺旋塞子的香槟。

9. 记得把马桶垫放下来。

10. 多数周末记得刮脸。

Age 52

1. Keeps hair in nose and ears trimmed to appropriate length.

2. Doesn't belch or scratch in public.

3. Doesn't borrow money too often.

4. Doesn't nod off to sleep while I'm emoting.

5. Doesn't re-tell the same joke too many times.

6. Is in good enough shape to get off the couch on weekends.

7. Usually wears matching socks and fresh underwear.

8. Appreciates a good TV dinner.

9. Remembers your name on occasion.

10. Shaves on some weekends.

52 岁时

1. 鼻毛和耳毛修剪到适当的长度。

2. 不会当众打嗝或是搔痒。

3. 不会过于频繁地借钱。

4. 不会在我滔滔不绝时打瞌睡。

5. 不会把同一个笑话讲无数遍。

6. 身体健康，至少周末能从沙发上爬起来。

7. 通常能穿上同一双的袜子和干净的内裤。

8. 爱吃电视便餐。

9. 有时能想起你的名字。

10. 隔几个周末会想起刮脸。

Age 62

1. Doesn't scare small children.

2. Remembers where the bathroom is.

3. Doesn't require much money for upkeep.

4. Only snores lightly when awake (LOUDLY when asleep).

5. Forgets why he's laughing.

6. Is in good enough shape to stand up alone.

7. Usually wears some clothes.

8. Likes soft foods.

9. Remembers where he left his teeth.

10. Remembers when.

62 岁时

1. 不会吓到小孩子。

2. 能找到洗手间。

3. 不需要太高的养护费用。

4. 醒着的时候只会发出轻微的鼾声（睡着时鼾声如雷）。

5. 不记得自己为什么发笑。

6. 身体健康，能够自己站起来。

7. 通常能够穿着些衣服蔽体。

8. 爱吃软食。

9. 记得自己把假牙放在哪里。

10. 记得……时候。

Age 72

1. Breathing. . . .

60

72 岁时

1. 会喘气……

☆ **trim** /trɪm/ *v.* 修剪

☆ **belch** /beltʃ/ *v.* 打嗝

☆ **nod off** 打瞌睡

☆ **emote** /ɪˈməʊt/ *v.* (演戏、拍电影等时)过火地表演;装模作样

How to Cross a River

One day three men were walking along and came upon a raging, violent river. They needed to get to the other side, but couldn't figure out how to cross it.

The first man prayed to God saying, "Please God, give me the strength, courage and ability to cross this river."

Poof! God gave him big arms and strong legs, and he was able to swim across the river in about two hours.

Seeing this, the second man prayed to God saying, "Please God, give me the strength, courage and ability to cross this river."

怎样过河

一天，三个男人走着走着来到一条湍急的河流前。他们要到河对岸去，却想不出怎样过河。

第一个人对上帝祷告道："上帝啊，请赐给我力量、勇气和能力让我渡过这条河。"

噗的一声——上帝给了他强壮的四肢，他在两个小时后游到了对岸。

看到这一切，第二个人对上帝祷告说："上帝啊，请赐给我力量、勇气和能力让我渡过这条河。"

Poof! God gave him the skill to chop down a tree and fashion it into a rowboat; he was able to row across the river in about one and a half hours.

The third man had seen how this worked out for the other two, so he also prayed to God saying, "Please God, give me the strength, courage and ability to cross this river."

Poof! God turned him into a woman, and he walked across the bridge.

噗的一声——上帝给了他伐木并把树干做成划艇的技术，他花了一个半小时划着船渡过了这条河。

第三个人看到了两个同伴的祈祷的作用，于是他也对上帝祷告道："上帝啊，请赐给我力量、勇气和能力让我渡过这条河。"

噗的一声——上帝把他变成了一个女人，他走上桥过了河。

☆ **raging** /ˈreɪdʒɪŋ/ *a.* 狂怒的；凶猛的；肆虐的

☆ **violent** /ˈvaɪələnt/ *a.* 强暴的；猛烈的，剧烈的

☆ **figure out**　计算出；想出；理解，明白

☆ **chop** /tʃɒp/ *v.* 砍；劈；斩；剁

☆ **fashion** /ˈfæʃn/ *v.* （常指用手工等）制作

☆ **rowboat** /ˈrəʊbəʊt/ *n.* 划艇

Cure for Unemployment

"So you think you could end all unemployment, do you?" asked the interviewer. "And how, if I may be so bold to inquire?"

"Why, I'd put all the men on one island and all the women on another." replied Paddy. "And what would they be doing then?"

"Building boats!"

男人与女人

解决失业问题的良方

"你认为你能够解决所有的失业问题，是吗?"采访者问道,"我想冒昧地问一句，怎么做?"

"是这样的，我要把所有的男人送到一个岛上，把所有的女人送到另一个岛上。"帕迪答道,"他们会做什么呢?"

"造船!"

Women's Language Translate

Yes. = No.

No. = Yes.

Maybe. = No.

I'm sorry. = You'll be sorry.

It's your decision. = The correct decision should be obvious by now.

Do what you want.... = You'll pay for this later.

Sure ... go ahead. = I don't want you to.

I'm not upset. = Of course I'm upset, you moron!

理解女人的话

好的。＝不好。

不好。＝好的。

也许吧。＝不好。

对不起。＝该道歉的人是你。

这是你的决定。＝到现在，正确的决定显而易见了吧。

做你想做的……＝然后你就会为此付出代价的。

当然，做吧。＝我不想让你那样做。

我没烦。＝我当然很烦，笨蛋。

You're so manly. = You need a shave and you sweat a lot.

Hang the picture there. = NO, I mean hang it there!

I heard a noise. = I noticed you were almost asleep.

Do you love me? = I'm going to ask for something expensive.

How much do you love me? = I did something today you're really not going to like.

I'll be ready in a minute. = Kick off your shoes and find a good game on TV.

Am I fat? = Tell me I'm beautiful.

你真有男人味。＝你该刮胡子了，而且你身上的汗味儿太重了。

把画挂在那儿。＝不，不，我是指挂在那边。

我听到有声音。＝我注意到你快睡着了。

你爱我吗？＝我想买件很贵的东西。

你有多爱我？＝今天我做了件你肯定不高兴我做的事。

我马上就好。＝脱掉鞋子找一档好看的节目看吧。

我胖吗？＝告诉我我很漂亮。

71

You have to learn to communicate. = Just agree with me.

Are you listening to me!? = Too late, you're dead.

I'm not yelling! = Yes I am yelling because I think this is important.

In response to "What's wrong?":

The same old thing. = Nothing.

Nothing. = Everything.

Nothing, really. = It's just that you're such an idiot!

男人与女人

你得学会交流。＝听我的就行。

你在听我说吗!? ＝太晚了，你完了！

我没在大叫！＝我是在大叫，因为我认为这很重要。

女人对"出什么事了?"的回答：

就那样。＝没事。

没事。＝我很有事。

真的没事。＝你简直是个白痴。

☆ moron /ˈmɔːrɒn/ n. 〈口〉蠢人，傻子，笨蛋

☆ manly /ˈmænlɪ/ a. 具有男子气概的；强壮的，勇
   敢的

73

Learning to Love

A guy noticed that his buddy was troubled and asked what was wrong.

"Oh, it's my girlfriend."

"Oh yeah? What's the problem?"

"When I asked her if she could learn to love me," he said, "she asked me how much I was willing to spend on her education."

学 会 爱

一个人注意到他的老朋友遇到了麻烦，就问他怎么回事。

"噢，是我的女朋友。"

"啊，你的女朋友怎么啦？"

"我对我的女朋友说让她学着爱我时，"朋友说，"她问我准备给她出多少学费。"

Feeling Sorry for Him

Two girls are having coffee when one notices that the other girl seems troubled and asks her, "Is something bugging you? You look anxious."

"Well, my boyfriend just lost all his money and life savings in the stock market," she explained.

"Oh, that's too bad," the other girl sympathized. "I'm sure you're feeling sorry for him."

"Yeah, I am," she said. "He'll miss me."

为他难过

两个女孩在喝咖啡，一个注意到另一个忧心忡忡的样子，于是问她："有什么事让你烦恼吗？你看起来焦虑不安。"

"是我的男朋友，他把所有的钱都赔在股市上了。"她解释说。

"噢，那可太糟了，"另一个表示了同情，"我知道你现在一定很为他难过。"

"是的，我当然为他难过，"她说，"他会想念我的。"

☆ **bug** /bʌg/ *v.* 〈美俚〉烦扰；使恼怒；使困惑
☆ **life savings** 一辈子的积蓄

Differences
Between Men and Women

Bathrooms

A man has 6 items in his bathroom: a toothbrush, toothpaste, shaving cream, a razor, a bar of Dial soap and a towel from a Holiday Inn.

The average number of items in a typical American women's bathroom is 437. A man would not be able to identify most of these items.

Going out

When a man says he is ready to go out, it means he is ready to go out.

男女间的差异

盥洗室里

一个男人通常只在盥洗室里放六件东西：牙刷、牙膏、剃须乳液、刮胡刀、香皂和一条从假日饭店拿回来的毛巾。

一个美国女人放在盥洗室里的东西的件数平均为437件，其中大多数的东西男人们都不知道是用来做什么的。

出门时

一个男人说他已经准备好要出去时，这就意味着他确实是准备好要出去了。

When a woman says she is ready to go out, it means she will be ready, as soon as she finds her other earring, makes one phone call and finishes putting on her makeup.

Cats

Women love cats.

Men say they love cats, but when women aren't looking, men abuse cats.

Shoes

When preparing for work, a woman will put on a Mondi wool suit, and then slip in Reebok sneakers. She will carry her dress shoes in a plastic bag from Sacks. When a woman gets to work, she will put on her dress shoes. Five minutes later she will kick them off because her feet are under the desk.

一个女人说她准备好要出去时，意味着她将要准备好。她还要找另一只耳环带上，还要打一个电话，还要化好妆。

对待猫的态度

女人爱猫。

男人声称他们爱猫，但是女人不注意时，他们会虐待猫。

关于穿鞋这件事

去上班时，女人会穿上名牌毛料套装，然后踩双锐步的运动鞋。她们把正装鞋放在塑料袋里。到了单位，女人换上正装鞋。5分钟以后，她们又会把鞋子踢掉，因为脚在桌子下面，没人看到。

A man will wear one pair of shoes for the entire day.

Nicknames

If Gloria, Suzanne, Debra and Michelle go out for lunch, they will call each other Gloria, Suzanne, Debra and Michelle.

But if Mike, Phil and Jack go out for a brew, they will affectionately refer to each other as Fat Boy, Peanut-Head and Useless.

Eating out

And when the check comes, Mike, Phil and Jack will each throw in $ 20 bills, even though it's only for $ 22.50. None of them will have anything smaller, and none will actually admit they want change back.

男人一整天都穿着同一双鞋子。

绰号的使用

格洛里亚、苏珊娜、黛布拉和米歇尔一块儿出去吃饭时，她们会称呼各自的名字。

迈克、菲尔和杰克一块儿出去喝一杯时，他们会无比亲热地叫各自的绰号：胖小子、木瓜脑袋和笨蛋。

吃饭付账时

侍者送来账单时，虽然饭钱只要 22 块 5 毛，迈克、菲尔和杰克却会每个人掏出 20 块钱来。他们谁都没有零钱，而且每个人都不要找钱。

When the girls get their check, out come the pocket calculators.

Groceries

A woman makes a list of things she needs and then goes out to the store and buys these things.

A man waits till the only items left in his fridge are half a lime and a soda. Then he goes grocery shopping. He buys everything that looks good. By the time a man reaches the checkout counter, his cart is packed tighter than the Clampett's car on Beverly Hillbillies. Of course, this will not stop him from going to the 10-items-or-less lane.

而姑娘们拿到账单时，会同时拿出小计算器。

去采购时

女人们出去采购前会列出一张所需购买物品的清单，然后去商店把它们买回来。

男人们要等到冰箱里只剩下半只酸橙和一瓶苏打水时，才会想起去商店。他们会把看起来不错的东西都买下。到收款台时，他的购物车上已经堆得满满当当了，当然，这也并不妨碍他去 10 件以下商品的快速通道交款。

Mirrors

Men are vain; they will check themselves out in the mirror.

Women are ridiculous; they will check out their reflections in any shiny surface, mirrors, spoons, store window and toasters.

The Telephone

Men see the telephone as a communication tool. They use the telephone to send short messages to other people.

A woman can visit her girlfriend for two weeks, and upon returning home, she will call the same friend and they will talk for three hours.

男人与女人

镜子的使用

男人们是爱美的，他们会在镜子前检视自己。

女人们是荒唐的，她们会从一切发亮的物体表面，镜子、勺子、商店橱窗甚至烤箱表面，检视自己。

关于电话

男人们认为电话就是联系工具，他们利用电话给他人传递简短的信息。

而一个女人却有可能在和女朋友一起待了两个星期后的回家路上打电话给这个女朋友，再聊上三个小时。

Directions

If a woman is out driving, and she finds herself in unfamiliar surroundings, she will stop at a gas station and ask for directions.

Men consider this to be a sign of weakness. Men will never stop and ask for directions. Men will drive in a circle for hours, all the while saying things like, "Looks like I've found a new way to get there." and, "I know I'm in the general neighborhood. I recognize that store."

Dressing up

A woman will dress up to: go shopping, water the plants, empty the garbage, answer the phone, read a book, get the mail.

A man will dress up for: weddings, funerals.

找不到方向时

一个女人开车外出时，当她来到一处不熟悉的地方时，她会找一个加油站问路。

男人们认为这是软弱无能的表现。他们决不会停下来问路，而是长时间地在附近兜圈子，并且不断地对自己说："看来我找到了一条新路。"或是"我知道我就在附近了，我认得那家商店。"

盛装的场合

女人们会精心打扮了去：逛街、浇花、倒垃圾、接电话、读书、收邮件。

男人会盛装出席：婚礼和葬礼。

Trips

If a man goes on a seven-day trip, he'll pack five days worth of clothes and will wear some things twice.

If a woman goes on a seven-day trip she'll pack 21 outfits because she doesn't know what she'll feel like wearing each day.

Toys

Little girls love to play with toys. Then when they reach the age of 11 or 12, they lose interest.

Men never grow out of their obsession with toys. As they get older, their toys simply

关于旅行

一个男人出去旅行七天，他会带五身衣服，然后把其中几件穿两次。

一个女人出去旅行七天，她会带二十一套衣服，因为她不知道自己第二天会想穿什么。

对待玩具的态度

小女孩们喜欢玩儿玩具。等她们长到十一二岁时，就会对玩具失去兴趣。

男人们永远钟情于玩具，只是随着年龄的增长，他们的玩具变得越来越贵且无用。

become more expensive and silly and impractical.

Examples of men's toys: little miniature TV's, car phones, complicated juicers and blenders, small robots that serve cocktails on command, video games, anything that blinks, beeps, and requires at least 6 batteries to operate.

Women never understand why men love toys.

Men understand that they wouldn't need toys if women had an "on/off" switch.

男人们的玩具如下：掌上电视、车载电话、复杂的榨汁机和搅拌器、能按指令送上鸡尾酒的小机器人、电视游戏。总之一切会发光的、发声的或是至少需要六节电池才能用的东西都会成为男人们的玩具。

女人永远不会理解男人为什么喜欢玩具。

男人们明白如果女人身上也有开关键的话，他们也就不需要那些东西了。

Offspring

Ah, children. A woman knows all about her children. She knows about dentist appointments and soccer games and romances and best friends and favorite foods and secret fears and hopes and dreams.

A man is vaguely aware of some short people living in the house.

Plants

A woman asks a man to water her plants while she is on vacation. The man waters the plants.

The woman comes home five or six days later to an apartment full of dead plants. No one knows why this happens.

对待孩子

噢，孩子们。女人了解孩子们的方方面面，包括牙医的预约时间、足球赛、恋爱经过、最好的朋友、最爱吃的东西、内心的恐惧、希望和梦想等等等等。

男人只是模模糊糊地知道家里有个小人。

植物的命运

女人在出去度假时要男人帮忙给植物浇水。男人照做了。

五六天后，女人回来发现满屋子的植物都死了。没人知道是怎么回事。

Mustaches

Some men look good with mustaches.

There are no women who look good with mustaches.

Cameras

Men take photography very seriously. They'll shell out $ 8000 for state of the art equipment, and build dark rooms and take photography classes.

Women purchase Kodak Instamatics.

Of course women always end up taking better pictures.

Locker Rooms

In the locker room men talk about three things: money, football and women. They exaggerate about money, they don't know

关于胡子

有些男人留起胡子来会很好看。

没有女人留胡子会好看。

相机的使用

男人对待摄影的态度是非常严肃认真的。他们会花上八千块钱买高档的设备、建专门的暗室，还报班学习摄影技术。

女人买柯达的傻瓜机。

当然最终是女人照出来的相片比较好。

衣帽间里的谈话

男人们聚在一起谈三件事：钱、足球和女人。说起钱来，他们夸大其实；说起足球，他们自以为是，其实不懂；他们编造关于女人的故事。

football nearly as well as they think they do, and they fabricate stories about women.

Women talk about one thing in the locker room — sex. And not in abstract terms, either. They are extremely graphic and technical, and they never lie.

Laundry

Women do the laundry every couple of days.

A man will wear every article of clothing he owns before he will do the laundry. When he is finally out of clothes, he will wear a dirty sweat suit inside out and take his mountain of dirty clothes to the Laundromat. Men always expect to meet beautiful women at the Laundromat, but this is only a myth perpetuated by old reruns of Love American Style.

女人们聚在一起只谈一件事：性。她们还不是泛泛而谈，而是绝对的生动形象，且决不说瞎话。

关于洗衣服这件事

女人每隔几天就洗一次衣服。

男人要把所有的衣服都穿遍了才会想到要洗衣服。到他没有衣服穿时，他会把一件脏兮兮满是汗臭的 T 恤翻过来套在身上，然后把他堆积如山的脏衣服送去洗衣店。男人们总是想在洗衣店碰到漂亮女人，然而这只是长久不衰的美国浪漫故事而已。

Politics

Men love to talk politics, but often they forget to do political things such as voting.

Women are very happy that another generation of Kennedy's is growing up and getting into politics because they will be able to campaign for them and cry on election night.

Weddings

When reminiscing about weddings women talk about "the ceremony."

Men talk about "the bachelor party."

Speeding Tickets

Women can get out of speeding tickets by pouting.

This will get men arrested.

关于政治

男人们热中于谈论政治，可他们经常忘记去参与政治事件，比如选举投票。

女人们很高兴肯尼迪家族的新一代已经成长起来，又可以为他们欢呼呐喊、摇旗助威了。

关于结婚

回忆起结婚的那段日子，女人说起的是婚礼。

男人说起的是单身聚会。

超速罚单

女人撅撅嘴就可以逃掉超速罚单。

男人这样做就会给抓起来。

☆ **abuse** /ə'bju:z/ *v.* 虐待，伤害

☆ **sneaker** /'sni:kə(r)/ *n.* (sneakers) 〈俚〉帆布胶底运动鞋，旅游鞋

☆ **affectionately** /ə'fekʃənətlɪ/ *ad.* 充满深情地

☆ **checkout** /'tʃekaʊt/ *n.* (超级市场等的) 付款台

☆ **vain** /veɪn/ *a.* 自负的；自视过高的；爱虚荣的

☆ **ridiculous** /rɪ'dɪkjʊləs/ *a.* 可笑的；荒唐的

☆ **reflection** /rɪ'flekʃən/ *n.* 映像，倒影

☆ **outfit** /'aʊtfɪt/ *n.* 全套衣服

☆ **obsession** /əb'seʃən/ *n.* 着迷；困扰

☆ **grow out of** 长大得与…不相称；因长大而丢弃

☆ **impractical** /ɪm'præktɪkəl/ *a.* 不切实际的；无用的

☆ **blink** /blɪŋk/ *v.* 眨眼睛；闪亮，闪烁

☆ **beep** /biːp/ *v.* 发出短促而尖利的声音

☆ **shell out** 交（款），付（款）

☆ **Instamatic** /ˌɪnstəˈmætɪk/ *n.* "傻瓜"照相机

☆ **locker room** （体育馆、俱乐部等的）衣物间；
（排斥外人的）小圈子聚会地

☆ **exaggerate** /ɪɡˈzædʒəreɪt/ *v.* 夸张，夸大

☆ **fabricate** /ˈfæbrɪkeɪt/ *v.* 编造（谎言、借口等）

☆ **abstract** /ˈæbstrækt/ *a.* 抽象的

☆ **graphic** /ˈɡræfɪk/ *a.* 生动的；轮廓分明的

☆ **Laundromat** /ˈlɔːndrəmæt/ *n.* （= launderette）
（装有投币洗衣机的）自助洗衣店

☆ **perpetuate** /pəˈpetjʊeɪt/ *v.* 使永久；使长存

☆ **rerun** /riːˈrʌn/ *n.* 重现，再次尝试

☆ **campaign** /kæmˈpeɪn/ *v.* 参加竞选

☆ **reminisce** /ˌremɪˈnɪs/ *v.* 回忆；话旧

☆ **pout** /paʊt/ *v.* 撅嘴；板脸，面露不悦

The Way You Say It

It's not what you say, but the way you say it.

On a blind date, the boy said to the girl, "Time stands still when I look into your eyes."

The girl was very flattered.

While what the boy had really meant was, "You have a face that would stop a clock."

你说话的方式

你说什么并不重要，重要的是你说话的方式。

在一次相亲中，男孩对女孩说："我看进你的眼睛时，时间停驻了。"

女孩听了很高兴。

然而男孩真正的意思是："你长着一张会让时钟停掉的脸。"

☆ **blind date**　（由第三方安排的）男女间初次会晤

☆ **flatter** /ˈflætə(r)/ v. 向…谄媚；使满足；使高兴

Correct Male Responses

What makes these questions so bad is that every one is guaranteed to explode into a major argument and/or divorce if the man does not answer properly.

Question 1: "Do you love me?"

The correct answer to this question is, "Yes." or if you want to be more elaborate, you may answer, "Yes, dear." Wrong answers include:

A. I suppose so.

B. Would it make you feel better if I said yes?

C. That depends on what you mean by "love."

D. Does it matter?

E. Who, me?

男人正确的回答

这些问题之所以说它们不好是因为每一个问题如果男人回答得不正确都会导致一场吵架甚至是离婚。

问题一："你爱我吗?"

正确的回答是:"爱。"如果你还想多说些,也可以说:"是的,亲爱的,我爱你。"错误的回答包括以下几种:

A. 我想是的。

B. 我说是你是不是会感觉好些?

C. 那得看你说的"爱"是什么意思。

D. 这很重要吗?

E. 谁,问我吗?

Question 2: "Do I look fat?"

The correct male response to this question is to confidently and emphatically state, "No, of course not!" and then quickly leave the room. Incorrect answers include:

A. I wouldn't call you fat, but you're not exactly thin.

B. Compared to what?

C. A little extra weight looks good on you.

D. I've seen fatter.

E. Could you repeat the question? I was just thinking about your insurance policy.

问题二："我看起来胖吗？"

正确的回答方式是确定无疑地说："不，你一点儿也不胖！"然后迅速离开房间。错误的回答包括以下几种：

A. 你这不叫胖，可也确实不太瘦。

B. 和谁比？

C. 你胖点儿好看。

D. 我看是胖了些。

E. 你再说一遍好吗？我刚刚在想你的保险条款。

Question 3: "Do you think she's prettier than me?"

The "she" in the question could be an ex-girlfriend, a passer-by you were staring at or anactress in a movie you just saw. In any case, the correct response is, "No, you are much prettier." or simply "Of course not!" Wrong answers include:

A. Not prettier, just pretty in a different way.

B. Not prettier, but definitely thinner.

C. Yes, but I bet you have a better personality.

D. Not as pretty as you when you were her age.

问题三:"你觉得她长得比我好看吗?"

这个问题中的"她"可能是你的前任女友或是你盯着看的一个过路人或是你们正在看的电影里的女演员。不管是谁,正确的回答是:"不,你要漂亮得多。"或者"当然没你漂亮!"错误的回答包括以下几种:

A. 并不比你漂亮,只是不同种类的漂亮。

B. 不比你漂亮,只是更苗条些。

C. 是的,但是我相信你的性格比她好。

D. 你在她这个年龄时你一定比她漂亮。

Question 4: "What would you do if I died?"

A definite no-win question. No matter how you answer this, be prepared for at least an hour of follow-up questions. This might be the stupidest question of the lot, as is illustrated by the following stupid exchange:

Woman: Dear, what would you do if I died?

Man: Why, dear, I would be extremely upset. Why do you ask such a question?

Woman: Would you get married again?

Man: No, of course not, dear.

Woman: Don't you like being married?

Man: Of course I do, dear.

Woman: Then why wouldn't you remarry?

Man: Alright, I'd remarry.

Woman: You would? (looking vaguely hurt)

问题四："我死了以后你会怎么办？"

这绝对是个没法回答的问题。不管你怎么回答，都要准备好回答至少一小时的后续问题。这是最愚蠢的问题，正如下面的对话展现的：

女人：亲爱的，我死了以后你会怎么办？

男人：亲爱的，我会非常伤心。你怎么会问这样的问题？

女人：你会再结婚吗？

男人：当然不会，亲爱的。

女人：你不喜欢婚姻吗？

男人：当然不是，亲爱的。

女人：那你为什么不想再结婚？

男人：好吧，我会再婚。

女人：你会？（看上去有些伤心）

Man: Yes.

Woman: Would you sleep with her in our bed?

Man: Well yes, I suppose I would. Where else would we sleep?

Woman: And would you take down the pictures of me and replace them with pictures of her? (icily)

Man: Yes. I think that would be the correct thing to do.

Woman: Is that so? (leaping to her feet) And I suppose you'd let her play with my golf clubs, too.

Man: Of course not, dear. She's left-handed. . . .

男人：是的。

女人：你会和她睡在我们的床上吗？

男人：是的，我想会的，不然我们睡哪儿？

女人：那么你会把我的照片都取下来换成她的吗？（冷冷地）

男人：是的，我想应该这样吧。

女人：是吗？（在跳脚儿了）我想你还会让她用我的高尔夫球杆吧。

男人：当然不，亲爱的，她是左撇子……

Question 5: What are you thinking about?

The proper answer to this, of course, is: "I'm sorry if I've been pensive, dear. I was just reflecting on what a warm, wonderful, thoughtful, caring, intelligent woman you are, and how lucky I am to have met you." Wrong answers include:

A. Baseball.

B. Football.

C. How fat you are.

D. How much prettier she is than you.

E. How I would spend the insurance money if you died.

问题五："你在想什么？"

正确的回答当然是："亲爱的，如果我显得心事重重，我只是在想你是一个热情、完美、细致而聪明的女人，我能和你在一起实在是很幸运。"错误的回答包括以下几种：

A. 棒球。

B. 足球。

C. 你太胖了。

D. 她比你漂亮多少。

E. 你死了以后我怎么花那笔保险费。

☆ **guarantee** /ˌgærən'tiː/ v.（事物）使（另一事物）必然发生，使变得确定

☆ **elaborate** /ɪ'læbərət/ a. 详尽的；精巧的

☆ **emphatically** /ɪm'fætɪkəlɪ/ ad. 强调地；断然地

☆ **pensive** /'pensɪv/ a. 冥想的；忧虑的

☆ **reflect on/upon** 深思；考虑；反省

Whom to Marry

There is a man who has three girlfriends, but he does not know which one to marry. So he decides to give each one of them $5000 and see how each of them spends it.

The first one goes out and gets a total makeover with the money. She gets new clothes, a new hairdo, manicure, pedicure, and tells the man, "I spent the money so I could look pretty for you because I love you so much."

The second one went out and bought new golf clubs, a CD player, a television, and

和谁结婚

有一个男人有三个女朋友，可是他不知道要和谁结婚好。于是他决定给她们每人五千块钱看她们都怎么花。

第一个女人用这笔钱把自己整个改头换面了一番。她买了新衣服，做了新发型，修了手指甲和脚。她对男人说："我把这些钱花在自己身上是为了让我更漂亮，从而更配你，这都是因为我很爱你。"

第二个女人用这些买了高尔夫球杆、CD 播放器、电视音响送给男人。她说："我买了这些东西送给你是因为我很爱你。"

stereo and gives them to the man. She says, "I bought these gifts for you because I love you so much."

The third one takes the $5000 and invests it in the stock market, doubles her investment, returns the $5000 and reinvests the rest. She says, "I am investing the rest of the money for our future because I love you so much."

The man thought long and hard about how each of the women spent the money, and decided to marry the one with the biggest breasts.

第三个女人拿了钱投入股市，又赚了五千块，她把五千块还给男人，用赚来的五千块继续投资。她说："我太爱你了，所以我用剩下的钱为我们以后的日子投资赚钱。"

男人长时间地仔细考虑了女人们的花钱方式，最后决定娶了那个胸最大的。

Perfect Man, Perfect Woman

There was a perfect man and a perfect woman. They met each other at a perfect party. They dated for two perfect years. They had the perfect wedding and the perfect honeymoon. They had two perfect children.

One day the perfect man and the perfect woman were driving in there perfect car, they saw Santa Claus at the side of the road, being the perfect people they picked him up, because they didn't want to make their perfect children (who were at home with their perfect babysitter) mad because it was close to Chritmas.

完美的男人，完美的女人

有一个完美的男人和一个完美的女人。他们在一个完美的晚会上相识了。他们完美地约会了两年。他们举行了完美的婚礼，度了完美的蜜月。他们有了两个完美的孩子。

一天，完美的男人和完美的女人正开着他们那辆完美的汽车在路上，他们看见圣诞老人站在路边。他们是完美的人，于是他们停下车带上圣诞老人。他们不想让待在家中由完美的保姆带着的完美的孩子们失望，因为圣诞节快到了。

Well as the perfect man and the perfect woman were driving with Santa Claus，somehow they got into an accident. Two people died and one lived.

Who died and who lived?

The perfect woman because the perfect man and Santa Claus aren't real.

可是，完美的男人和完美的女人载上圣诞老人后出了车祸。两个人死了，一个人活了下来。

谁死了，谁活了？

完美的女人活了，因为完美的男人和圣诞老人都是不存在的。

☆ **pick up** （停下来）把（人或东西）带走（或取走），把…载上车（或船等）

Rules Guys Wish Women Knew!

1. If you think you are fat, you probably are. Do not ask us. We refuse to answer.

2. Learn to work the toilet seat. If it's up, Put it down.

3. Do not cut your hair. Ever. Long hair is always more attractive than short hair. One of the big reasons guys fear getting married is that married women always cut their hair, and by then, you are stuck with her.

4. Birthdays, Valentines, and Anniversaries are not quests to see if we can find the perfect present!

5. If you ask a question you don't want an answer to, expect an answer you do not want to hear.

男人与女人

女人能了解这些规则多好啊！

1. 如果你们认为自己胖了，那么你们也许就是胖了，不要来问我们，我们拒绝回答。

2. 学会使用马桶坐垫，如果坐垫抬起来了，自己放下来吧。

3. 不要剪头发，永远不要。长头发总是比短头发有魅力。男人们害怕结婚的一个重要因素就是已婚女人总会剪短头发，然后你就不得不和她粘在一起了。

4. 生日、情人节和纪念日并不是用来考察我们能否找到完美的礼物的！

5. 如果你问一个不需要答案的问题，就等着听一个你不想要的回答吧。

127

6. Sometimes, we are not thinking about you. Live with it.

7. Do not ask us what we are thinking about unless you are prepared to discuss such topics as the shotgun formation and monster trucks.

8. Sunday = sports. It's like the full moon or the changing of the tides. Let it be.

9. Shopping is not a sport, and no, we are never going to think of it that way.

10. Anything you wear is fine. Really.

11. You have enough clothes.

12. You have too many shoes.

13. Crying is blackmail. Use it if you must, but don't expect us to like it.

6. 我们有时不会想到你们，忍一忍吧。

7. 不要问我们在想什么，除非你们想一起讨论橄榄球或巨型卡车。

8. 星期天就是运动时间，就像是满月或潮汐。你别想改变什么。

9. 逛街不是运动，不，我们永远都不会那么想。

10. 你穿什么都好看，真的。

11. 你的衣服足够多了。

12. 你的鞋子太多了。

13. 哭是一种胁迫方式，你可以在必要的时候使用，可别指望我们会喜欢。

14. Your ex-boyfriend is an idiot.

15. Ask for what you want. Let us be clear on this one: Subtle hints do not work. Strong hints do not work. Obvious hints do not work. Just say it!

16. Yes and No are perfectly acceptable answers to almost every question.

17. Come to us with a problem only if you want help solving it. That is what we do. Sympathy is what your girlfriends are for.

18. A headache that lasts for 17 months is a problem. See a doctor.

19. Foreign films are best left to foreigners.

20. Check your oil.

21. Women wearing Wonderbras and low-cut blouses lose their right to complain about having their boobs stared at.

14. 你的前任男友是个白痴。

15. 你们想要什么就直说！隐晦的暗示没用，强烈的暗示没用，明显的暗示也没用，就直说吧！

16. "是"和"不是"几乎能够回答所有的问题。

17. 带着你想要解决的问题来找我们，我们能做的是解决它。如果你们想要同情和安慰，去找你们的女朋友。

18. 持续了 17 个月的头痛是个大问题，去看医生。

19. 外国的电影最好留给外国人看吧。

20. 检查你的油箱。

21. 穿着魔术胸衣和低胸上衣的女人们没权利抱怨我们盯着她们的胸部看。

22. More women should wear Wonderbras and low-cut blouses. We like staring at boobs.

23. The relationship is never going to be like it was the first two months we were going out.

24. Beer is as exciting for us as handbags are for you.

25. If it is OUR house, I do not understand why MY stuff gets thrown in the closet or attic or basement.

26. We are not mind readers and we never will be. Our lack of mind-reading ability is not proof of how little we care about you.

27. If we ask what is wrong and you say "nothing," we will act like nothing's wrong. We know you are lying, but it is just not worth the hassle.

22. 应该有更多的女人穿上魔术胸衣和低胸上衣，我们喜欢看她们。

23. 我们的关系永远不可能再像我们刚开始约会的两个月时那样了。

24. 啤酒会让我们兴奋就像你们见到新手袋一样。

25. 如果这是我们的房子，我就不明白为什么我的东西要被扔进抽屉、阁楼或是地下室里。

26. 我们不能看透别人的心思，而且以后也不会。我们没有这种能力并不能说明我们不关心你们。

27. 如果我们问你们怎么啦，而你们回答"没事"，那我们就会装作没事的样子。我们知道你们在说谎，只是没必要为这个争论一番。

28. Get rid of your cat. And no, it's not different, it's just like ever other cat.

29. Dogs are better than ANY cats. Period.

30. Your Mom doesn't have to be our best friend.

31. Don't give us 50 rules when 25 will do.

32. Telling us that the models in the men's magazines are airbrushed makes you look jealous and petty, and it's certainly not going to deter us from reading the magazines.

33. Never buy a "new" brand of beer because "it was on sale."

34. If we're in the backyard and the TV in the den is on, that doesn't mean we're not watching it.

28. 处理掉你的猫。不，这都一样，它和别的猫没什么两样。

29. 狗就是比哪种猫都好。

30. 你妈妈没必要成为我们最好的朋友。

31. 如果二十五条规定就足够了，那就不要给我们五十条。

32. 告诉我们杂志上那些模特的身材都是用电脑修出来的不但使你们显得嫉妒又小气，而且也不会吓得我们不再看那些杂志。

33. 不要仅仅因为"特卖"就买回来一种没听说过的啤酒。

34. 房间里的电视开着而我们人在后院里并不意味着我们没在看电视。

35. Don't tell anyone we can't afford a new car. Tell them we don't want one.

36. Please don't drive when you're not driving.

37. When the waiter asks if everything's okay, a simple "Yes" is fine.

35. 不要告诉别人我们买不起新车，要说我们不想买。

36. 你不开车的时候就不要指手画脚了。

37. 服务生来问意见时，只要简单地说"好"就行了。

☆ **shotgun formation**（美式橄榄球的枢纽前卫在争球线后，其他后卫向两侧分开的）拉开进攻阵式

☆ **headache** /ˈhedeɪk/ *n.* 头痛；〈口〉令人头痛的事（或人）；麻烦事

☆ **hassle** /ˈhæsl/ *n.* 激烈而持久的争论；争吵

☆ **period** /ˈpɪərɪəd/ *int.* 〈美口〉[常用于叙述事实或看法后表示强调] 就是这话；就是这么回事

Something Real Cheap

After being away on business for a week before Christmas, Tom thought it would be nice to bring his wife a little gift.

"How about some perfume?" he asked the cosmetics clerk.

She showed him a bottle costing $ 50.

"That's a bit much," said Tom, so she returned with a smaller bottle for $ 30.

"That's still quite a bit," Tom groused.

Growing disgusted, the clerk brought out a tiny $ 15 bottle.

Tom grew agitated, "What I mean," he said, "is I'd like to see something real cheap."

So the clerk handed him a mirror!

真正便宜的东西

汤姆在圣诞节前出差了一个星期，回来时他想最好给妻子带一件小礼物。

"香水怎么卖？"他问卖化妆品的售货员。

她拿给他一瓶 50 元的香水。

"有点儿太贵了，"汤姆说。她给他换了一个小瓶 30 元的。

"还是有点儿贵，"汤姆抱怨道。

售货员有些烦他了，给他拿了一小瓶 15 元的。

汤姆烦躁地说："我想要的是真正便宜的东西。"

于是，售货员拿给他一面镜子！

☆ **grouse** /graʊs/ *v.* 抱怨，发牢骚

☆ **disgusted** /dɪsˈɡʌstɪd/ *a.* 厌恶的；愤慨的

☆ **agitated** /ˈædʒɪteɪtɪd/ *a.* 狂躁不安的；焦虑的

☆ **cheap** /tʃiːp/ *a.* 廉价的，便宜的；吝啬的，小气的

The Perfect Mate

At a local coffee bar, a young woman was expounding on her idea of the perfect mate to some of her friends.

"The man I marry must be a shining light amongst company. He must be musical. Tell jokes. Sing. And stay home at night!"

A cynical male listener overheard and spoke up, "Lady, if that's all you want, get a television set!"

男人与女人

完美的伴侣

在当地的一个咖啡吧里，一个年轻女士正在对朋友们讲述自己对完美伴侣的要求。

"我要嫁的人一定要是人杰。他要有音乐天赋，要有幽默感，会唱歌。晚上要留在家里陪我！"

一个刻薄的男人在旁边听到了她的话，大声说道："女士，如果这就是你想要的，去买一台电视吧！"

☆ **expound** /ɪkˈspaʊnd/ *v.* 详述，阐述；说明，讲解

☆ **shining light** 杰出的人，人杰

☆ **amongst** /əˈmʌŋst/ *prep.* (＝among) 在…的一类中；突出于…类型中；在…范围之内

☆ **cynical** /ˈsɪnɪkəl/ *a.* 挑剔挖苦的，冷嘲热讽的

☆ **overhear** /ˌəʊvəˈhɪə(r)/ *v.* 无意中听到，偶然听到

141

Keep Your Seat

A radical feminist is getting on a bus when, just in front of her, a man gets up from his seat.

She thinks to herself, "Here's another man trying to keep up the customs of a patriarchal society by offering a poor, defenseless woman his seat," and she pushes him back onto the seat.

A few minutes later, the man tries to get up again. She is insulted again and refuses to let him up.

Finally, the man says, "Look, lady, you've got to let me get up. I'm two miles past my stop already!"

男人与女人

(142)

留着你的座位吧

一个极端女权主义者上了一辆公共汽车，她面前的一个男人从他的座位上站了起来。

女权主义者想："这又是个试图通过给一个可怜的、无助的女人让座来维系男权社会旧习俗的人。"于是，她把他推回到座位上。

几分钟后，他又站了起来。她觉得受到了侮辱，于是又不让他站起来。

终于，他说："女士，你得让我站起来，我已经坐过站有两里路了。"

☆ **radical** /ˈrædɪkəl/ *a.* 极端的；激进的

☆ **feminist** /ˈfemɪnɪst/ *n.* 男女平等主义者

☆ **patriarchal** /ˌpeɪtrɪˈɑːkəl/ *a.* 家长（制）的；父权制的

☆ **defenseless** /dɪˈfenslɪs/ *a.* 无保护的，不能自卫的

143

Facts About Women

男人与女人

1. Women love to shop. It is the one area of the world where they feel like they're actually in control.

2. Women especially love a bargain. The question of "need" is irrelevant, so don't bother pointing it out.

3. Women never have anything to wear. Don't question the racks of clothes in the closet; you "just don't understand."

4. Women need to cry. And they won't do it alone unless they know you can hear them.

5. Women will always ask questions that have no right answer, in an effort to trap you into

有关女人的事实

1. 女人爱去商场购物，商场是她们认为在这个世界上她们能够实际控制的区域。

2. 女人都喜欢特价商品，所谓的"需求"是无关紧要的，就没必要给她们指出来了。

3. 女人总是没衣服穿，不用问她们壁橱里挂的那些衣服是怎么回事，你"就是不会明白的"。

4. 女人是要哭的，而且她们自己哭的时候一定会让你听到。

5. 女人总是要问没有正确答案的问题，就是为了要让你感到内疚。

feeling guilty.

6. Women love to talk. Silence intimidates them and they feel a need to fill it, even if they have nothing to say.

7. Women need to feel like there are people worse off than they are. That's why soap operas and Oprah Winfrey-type shows are so successful.

8. Women hate bugs. Even the strong-willed ones need a man around when there's a spider or a wasp involved.

9. Women can't keep secrets. They eat away at them from the inside. And they don't view it as being untrustworthy, providing they only tell two or three people.

6. 女人爱说个不停，沉默会让她们感觉受到威胁，所以一定要打破它，即使他们没什么可说的。

7. 女人需要知道有人比她们生活得不好，这就是肥皂剧和奥普拉脱口秀风行一时的原因所在。

8. 女人都讨厌昆虫，再强势的女人见到蜘蛛或是黄蜂之类的虫子也要男人在旁保护。

9. 女人不能保守秘密，这些东西会让她们内心痒痒的。而且如果只对两三个人说起，她们也不认为这是泄密。

10. Women always go to public restrooms in groups. It gives them a chance to gossip.

11. Women think all beer is the same.

12. Women keep three different shampoos and two different conditioners in the shower.

13. After a woman showers, the bathroom will smell like a tropical rain forest.

14. Women brush their hair BEFORE bed.

15. Women are NEVER wrong. Apologizing is the man's responsibility.

16. Women do NOT know anything about cars. "Oil-stick? Oil doesn't stick."

10. 女人总是结伴去洗手间，并趁此机会交头接耳。

11. 女人觉得所有的啤酒都一个味。

12. 女人会在浴室里放上三种洗发水和两种护发素。

13. 女人洗完澡后，浴室就像是热带雨林。

14. 女人在睡觉前梳头。

15. 女人从来不会出错，道歉是男人的义务。

16. 女人对车一无所知。"油穿刺（机油尺）？油不会穿刺的。"

17. Women will drive miles out of their way to avoid the possibility of getting lost using a shortcut.

18. Women do NOT want an honest answer to the question, "How do I look?"

19. Women will make three right-hand turns to avoid making one left-hand turn.

20. "Oh, nothing," has an entirely different meaning in woman-language than it does in man-language.

21. Women cannot use a map without turning the map to correspond to the direction that they are heading.

17. 女人开车在路上时，会为了怕抄近路迷了路而绕上几里远。

18. 对于"我看上去怎么样"之类的问题，女人并不想要你诚实地回答。

19. 为了避免左拐弯，女人会来三个右拐弯。

20. "哦，没什么"这句话从女人嘴里说出来的含义和从男人嘴里说出来的大相径庭。

21. 女人一定要把地图的方向和地理方位对应上才能看得懂地图。

22a. All women are overweight by definition, don't argue with them about it.

22b. All women are overweight by definition, don't agree with them about it.

23. If it is not Valentine's Day, and you see a man in a flower shop, you can probably start up a conversation by asking, "What did you do?"

22a. 理论上讲，所有的女人都超重，在这一点上不要和她们争论。

22b. 理论上讲，所有的女人都超重，在这一点上不要附和她们。

23. 如果你在不是情人节的时候看到一个男人在花店里，就几乎一定可以问他："你做了什么？"

☆ **irrelevant** /ɪˈreləvənt/ *a.* 不重要的；不相关的

☆ **intimidate** /ɪnˈtɪmɪdeɪt/ *v.* 恫吓，恐吓，威胁

☆ **eat away at**　烦扰

☆ **untrustworthy** /ˌʌnˈtrʌstˌwɜːðɪ/ *a.* 不可信赖的

Who Are You?

男人与女人

A man really loved a woman, but he was just too shy to propose to her.

Now he was up in his years and neither of them had ever been married.

Of course, they dated about once a week for the past six years, but he was so timid he just never got around to suggesting marriage.

But one day, he became determined to ask her the question.

So he calls her on the phone, "June."

"Yes, this is June."

"Will you marry me?"

"Of course I will! Who's this?"

你 是 谁?

一个男人深爱着一个女人,可是他太羞涩了,不敢向她求婚。

现在他上了岁数,他们两人都没结婚。

当然,在过去的六年中,他们每个星期都会约会一次。但是他就是太胆小了,从来也没提起过结婚的事。

终于有一天,他决定向她求婚。

于是他打电话给她:"是琼吗。"

"我就是。"

"你愿意嫁给我吗?"

"当然,我愿意!你是谁?"

☆ **propose** /prəˈpəuz/ *v.* (常指男子)求婚

You Know the History

Adam was walking around the Garden of Eden feeling very lonely, so God asked him, "What is wrong with you?"

Adam said he didn't have anyone to talk to.

God said that He was going to make Adam a companion and that it would be a woman.

He said, "This person will gather food for you, cook for you, and when you discover clothing she'll wash it for you.

"She will always agree with every decision you make.

"She will bear your children and never ask you to get up in the middle of the night to take care of them.

你知道的历史

亚当孤独地在伊甸园里游荡，上帝问他："你怎么啦?"

亚当说没有人陪他说话。

于是上帝说要给他造一个伴——一个女人。

上帝说："女人会为你采集食物，给你做饭，你发现做衣服的材料时，她会帮你洗。"

"她会同意你做出的每个决定。"

"她会为你生孩子，而且不用你半夜爬起来照顾他们。"

"She will not nag you and will always be the first to admit she was wrong when you've had a disagreement.

"All in all, she will enjoy being with you."

Adam asked God, "What will a woman like this cost?"

God replied, "An arm and a leg."

Then Adam asked, "What can I get for a rib?"

The rest is history. . . .

男人与女人

"她不会对你喋喋不休，在你们有不同意见时，她总会先承认错误。"

"总之，她很享受和你在一起。"

亚当问上帝："这样的女人要我付出什么代价？"

上帝答道："一只胳臂和一条腿。"

亚当问："我用一根肋骨能得到什么？"

后面的事情你们都知道了……

Comparing Men/Women at the ΛTM . . .

Instructions for the guys:

1. Pull up to ATM

2. Insert Card

3. Enter PIN

4. Take cash, card and receipt

5. Drive away

Instructions for the Gals:

1. Pull up to ATM

2. Back up and pull forward to get closer

3. Shut off engine

男人和女人在提款机前

男人的步骤：

1. 把车开到提款机前

2. 插卡

3. 输入密码

4. 取出现金、卡和取款凭条

5. 开车离开

女人的步骤：

1. 把车开到提款机前

2. 倒车然后再往前开好离提款机更近些

3. 熄火

4. Put keys in purse

5. Get out of car because you're too far from machine

6. Hunt for card in purse

7. Insert card

8. Enter PIN

9. Study instructions

10. Hit "CANCEL"

11. Re-enter correct PIN

12. Check balance

13. Make cash withdrawal

14. Take card and receipt

15. Get in car

16. Put card and receipt in wallet

17. Clear area in purse for wallet

4. 把钥匙放进包里

5. 从车里出来，因为还是离提款机太远

6. 在包里找卡

7. 插卡

8. 输入密码

9. 查看说明文字

10. 按"取消"键

11. 输入正确的密码

12. 查询余额

13. 取现

14. 取回卡和取款凭条

15. 回到车里

16. 把卡和取款凭条放进钱包

17. 把钱包塞进包里

18. Check makeup

19. Start car

20. Check makeup

21. Put car in reverse

22. Put car in drive

23. Drive 3 miles

24. Release parking brake

男人与女人

18. 照镜子检查妆容

19. 发动车子

20. 照镜子检查妆容

21. 倒车

22. 开上车行道

23. 开出三里地

24. 松手刹

Without Woman

A women's lib speaker was addressing a large group and said, "Where would man be today if it were not for woman?"

She paused a moment and looked around the room.

"I repeat, where would man be today if it were not for woman?"

From the back of the room came a voice . . . "He'd still be in the Garden of Eden eating strawberries!"

没有女人

一个妇女解放运动演说家正在对一大群人发表演说，她问道："如果没有女人，男人现在会在哪儿呢？"

她停了一下，环顾四周。

"我再说一遍，如果没有女人，男人现在会在哪儿呢？"

房间的后面传来一个人的声音："他还会待在伊甸园里吃草莓!"

What's a Man?

One day in the Garden of Eden, Eve calls out to God.

"Lord, I have a problem!"

"What's the problem, Eve?"

男人与女人

"Lord, I know you created me and provided this beautiful garden and all of these wonderful animals and that hilarious comedic snake, but I'm just not happy."

"Why is that, Eve?" came the reply from above.

"Lord, I am lonely, and I'm sick to death of apples."

"Well Eve, in that case, I have a solution. I shall create a man for you."

男人是什么？

一天在伊甸园里，夏娃叫住了上帝。

"上帝，我有个麻烦！"

"你怎么啦，夏娃？"

"上帝，我知道你创造了我，还给我准备了这么美丽的花园，所有这些好棒的动物和那条滑稽的蛇，可是我并不幸福。"

"为什么呢？"上帝问。

"上帝，我很孤独，而且我太想吃苹果了。"

"那么，夏娃，我有一个办法，我为你创造一个男人。"

169

"What's a man, Lord?"

"Man will be a flawed creature, with many bad traits. He'll lie, cheat and be vainglorious; all in all, he'll give you a hard time.

"But ... he'll be bigger, faster, and will like to hunt and kill things. He will look silly when he's aroused.

"He will be witless and will revel in childish things like fighting and kicking a ball about.

"He won't be too smart, so he'll also need your advice to think properly."

"Sounds great!" says Eve, with an ironically raised eyebrow.

"Well ... you can have him on one condition."

170

"上帝，男人是什么？"

"男人是一种有缺陷的生物，他有很多不好的习性，他会撒谎、欺骗还夸夸其谈。总之，和他在一起你会很难过。"

"但是他的身材比你高大，速度也比你快，还喜欢猎杀。他生气的时候看起来会很愚蠢。"

"他会失去理智，沉迷于一些幼稚的事情，比如打打闹闹或是把球踢来踢去什么的。"

"他不大聪明，会需要你的忠告。"

"听起来不错嘛！"夏娃扬了扬眉毛，嘲讽地说。

"只是……有一个条件。"

171

"What's that, Lord?"

"As I said, he'll be proud, arrogant and self-admiring. . . .

"So you'll have to let him believe that I made him first.

"Just remember, it's our little secret . . . .

"You know, woman to woman."

172

"什么条件?"

"正如我说过的，他骄傲、自大又自负……"

"所以你要让他认为我是先创造了他。"

"记得这是我们的小秘密……"

"你知道，女人间的小秘密。"

☆ **hilarious** /hɪˈleərɪəs/ *a.* 兴高采烈的；滑稽的

☆ **comedic** /kəˈmiːdɪk/ *a.* 关于喜剧的；滑稽的

☆ **flaw** /flɔː/ *v.* 使有缺陷

☆ **vainglorious** /ˌveɪnˈglɔːrɪəs/ *a.* 十分自负的

☆ **arrogant** /ˈærəgənt/ *a.* 傲慢的；自大的

It's Better to Be a Woman!

1. We got off the Titanic first.

2. Our boyfriend's clothes make us look elfin & gorgeous. Guys look like complete idiots in ours.

3. We can cry and get off speeding fines.

4. We've never lusted after a cartoon character or the central female figure in a computer game.

5. Men die earlier, so we get to cash in on the life insurance.

6. Free drinks, Free dinners, Free movies. . . .

7. We can hug our friends without wondering if she thinks we're gay.

8. We can hug our friends without wondering if WE're gay.

还是做女人比较好！

1. 我们优先从泰坦尼克号上下来。

2. 我们穿上男朋友的衣服显得小巧可爱；他们穿上我们的衣服完全是一副白痴相。

3. 我们掉掉眼泪就能躲掉超速罚单。

4. 我们从不会去贪恋一个卡通形象或是电脑游戏里的女主角。

5. 男人的寿命比较短，所以是我们能领到寿险保险金。

6. 免费吃喝，免费看电影……

7. 我们可以尽管去拥抱我们的朋友，而不用担心她会认为我们俩是同性恋。

8. 我们可以尽管去拥抱我们的朋友，而不用怀疑我们自己是同性恋。

9. New lipstick gives us a whole new lease on life.

10. If we have a zit, we know how to conceal it.

11. We have the ability to dress ourselves.

12. Our friends won't think we're weird if we ask whether there's spinach in our teeth.

13. There are times when chocolate really can solve all your problems.

14. We can fully assess a person just by looking at their shoes.

15. We have enough sense to realize that the easiest way to get out of being lost is to ask for directions.

9. 一款新口红就能让我们享受到愉快的新生活。

10. 长了青春痘，我们知道怎么把它藏起来。

11. 我们会把自己装扮好。

12. 当我们问朋友们我们的牙缝里有没有菠菜时，她们不会认为我们有病。

13. 有时巧克力确实能解决我们所有的问题。

14. 看一个人穿的鞋子我们就能看出他是什么样的人。

15. 我们很明智地知道解决迷路问题最简便的方法就是找人问路。

☆ **elfin** /ˈelfɪn/ *a.* 活泼淘气的；小巧的

☆ **cash in on** 靠⋯赚钱，从⋯中捞到好处

☆ **a new lease on life** （大病痊愈或烦恼消除后）愉快和更有生气的新生活

☆ **weird** /wɪəd/ *a.* 怪诞的；奇特的；不可思议的

She Could Love You

One day, Adam sat outside the Garden of Eden shortly after eating the apple, and wondered about men and women. So looking up to the heavens he says, "Excuse me God, can I ask you a few questions?"

God replied, "Go on Adam but be quick I have a world to create."

So Adam says, "When you created Eve, why did You make her body so curvy and tender unlike mine?"

"I did that, Adam, so that you could love her."

她 会 爱 你

一天，亚当吃完苹果坐在伊甸园外，对男人和女人的问题感到迷惑不解，于是他抬头望天，说："上帝，打扰了，我能问几个问题吗?"

上帝答道："亚当，你问吧，不过要快点儿，我还要创世呢。"

于是亚当问道："你创造夏娃时，为什么把她造得柔软而凹凸有致，和我不一样?"

"亚当，我这样做是为了让你能爱上她。"

"Oh, well then, why did You give her long, shiny, beautiful hair, and not me?"

"I did that Adam so that you could love her."

"Oh, well then, why did You make her so stupid? Certainly not so that I could love her?"

"Well Adam, no. I did that so that she could love you!"

"哦，那么你为什么给她闪亮的、漂亮的长发，而不给我呢?"

"亚当，我这样做是为了让你能爱上她。"

"哦，那么你为什么把她造得傻乎乎的呢? 这肯定不会是为了让我能爱上她吧?"

"当然不是，亚当，我这样做是为了让她能爱上你!"

I'll Wait for the Police

A woman and a man were involved in a car accident — it was a bad one. Both of their cars were totally demolished, but amazingly, neither of them were hurt.

After they crawled out of their cars, the woman said, "So, you're a man — that's interesting. I'm a woman. Wow, just look at our cars! There's nothing left, but fortunately we are both unhurt. This must be a sign from God that we should meet and be friends, and live together in peace for the rest of our days."

The man thoughtfully replied, "I agree with you completely. This must be a sign from God!"

我要等警察来

一个男人和一个女人的车撞到了一起，撞得很严重，两个人的车全都面目全非。令人称奇的是他们两个人竟然都没事。

从各自的车里爬出来后，女人说："这么说你是个男人，太有意思了，我是个女人。哦，看看我们的车，完全报废了，可幸运的是，我们都没事。这一定是上帝的意旨，要我们相识相知，并在今后的日子里和睦地生活在一起。"

男人想了想答道："我完全同意你说的，这一定是上帝的意旨！"

The woman continued, "And look at this, here's another miracle. My car is completely demolished but this bottle of wine didn't break. Surely God wants us to drink this wine and celebrate our good fortune."

Then she handed the bottle to the man. The man nodded his head in agreement, opened it, and drank half the bottle. He then handed it back to the woman. The woman took the bottle, and immediately put the cork back in, and handed it back to the man.

In surprise, he asked, "Aren't you having any?"

"No," the woman replied, "I think I'll just wait for the police...."

184

女人接着说道："看这个，这是又一个奇迹嘛，我的车已经撞烂了，可这瓶酒竟然没有碎。一定是上帝要我们用它来庆贺一下我们的好运。"

她把那瓶酒递给男人。男人点点头，打开瓶塞，喝了半瓶，递回给女人。女人拿过酒瓶，马上把瓶塞盖好，又递给了男人。

男人很诧异，问道："你不来点儿吗？"

"不，"女人答道，"我想我还是等警察来好了……"

You Are the Only Woman

Adam was returning home late one night at paradise after drinking with the dodo and the unicorn. Eve got angry and yelled at him, "YOU ARE SEEING ANOTHER WOMAN!"

Adam responded, "Don't be silly, you are the only woman on earth." and went to sleep.

Later that night Adam woke up, feeling a tickle in his chest and saw it was Eve. "What the heck are you doing?" he asked.

"I'm counting your ribs!" she responded.

男人与女人

你是惟一的女人

一天晚上，亚当和渡渡鸟还有独角兽去喝酒，回家晚了。夏娃很生气，对他叫道："你看上了别的女人！"

亚当答道："别傻了，你是这里惟一的女人。"然后就去睡了。

半夜时，亚当醒来，觉得胸口痒痒，发现是夏娃在指指戳戳。"你到底在干吗？"

"我在数你的肋骨！"

Keep Your Photo

A soldier serving overseas far from home was annoyed and upset when his girl wrote to break off their engagement and ask for her photograph back.

He went out and collected from his friends all the unwanted photographs of women that he could find, bundled them all together, and sent them back with a note saying, "I regret that I cannot remember which one you are. Please keep your photo and return the others."

留下你的照片

一个士兵在海外服役时，未婚妻来信要和他断绝关系并要回自己的照片，他对此很生气和烦恼。

于是他去朋友们那儿搜集来他们不要了的女人照片，打包寄给未婚妻。包里附有一张字条写着："很遗憾我记不得你是谁了，请留下你的照片，然后把其他的寄回给我。"

Conversations

Husband: I hear that fish is good for our brain.

Wife: You had better eat a whale.

Ann: How long can a person live without brains?

Billy: I don't know. How old are you?

Father: Don't you think our son gets all his brains from me?

Mother: Probably. I still have all mine.

Tim: She's a bright girl ... she has brains enough for two.

几段对话

丈夫：我听说鱼很补脑。

妻子：那你最好吃鲸鱼。

安：一个人没有脑子能活多久？

比利：我不知道。你多大了？

父亲：你不觉得我们的儿子完全遗传了我的智慧吗？

母亲：也许吧，我的还都在。

蒂姆：她是个聪明的女孩，她脑袋好使。

Ray: Then she's just the girl for you.

Tom: Why do women have smaller feet than men?

Jim: So they can stand closer to the sink.

John: Did you hear they finally made a device that makes cars run 95% quieter?

Gall: Yeah, it fits right over her mouth.

雷：那她很适合你。

汤姆：为什么女人的脚比男人的小？

吉米：这样才好离水池近些。

约翰：你听说了吗，他们终于造出了能让汽车降噪95％的装置了？

高尔：听说了，装在她嘴上最合适。